HISTORY'S GREATEST RIVALS

CLEOPATRA Vs. THE ROMAN EMPIRE

POWER, CONQUEST, AND TRAGEDY

Ellis Roxburgh

Gareth Stevens
PUBLISHING

Please visit our website, **www.garethstevens.com**.
For a free color catalog of all our high-quality books,
call toll free 1-800-542-2595 or fax 1-877-542-2596.

Library of Congress Cataloging-in-Publication Data

Roxburgh, Ellis, author.
  Cleopatra vs. the Roman empire : power, conquest, and tragedy / Ellis Roxburgh.
     pages cm. — (History's greatest rivals)
  Includes index.
  ISBN 978-1-4824-4223-6 (pbk.)
  ISBN 978-1-4824-4224-3 (6 pack)
  ISBN 978-1-4824-4225-0 (library binding)
  1. Cleopatra, Queen of Egypt, -30 B.C.—Juvenile literature. 2. Egypt—
History—332-30 B.C.—Juvenile literature. 3. Rome—History—Republic, 265-30 B.C.—
Juvenile literature. 4. Rome—History—Augustus, 30 B.C.-14 A.D.—Juvenile literature.
5. Egypt—Relations—Rome—Juvenile literature. 6. Rome—Relations—Egypt—Juvenile
literature.
  I. Title. II. Title: Cleopatra versus the Roman empire.
  DT92.7.R69 2016
  932'.021—dc23

                                         2015027020

Published in 2016 by
Gareth Stevens Publishing
111 East 14th Street, Suite 349
New York, NY 10003

Copyright © 2016 Brown Bear Books Ltd

For Brown Bear Books Ltd:
Editorial Director: Lindsey Lowe
Managing Editor: Tim Cooke
Children's Publisher: Anne O'Daly
Design Manager: Keith Davis
Designer: Lynne Lennon
Picture Manager: Sophie Mortimer

Picture Credits: T=Top, C=Center, B=Bottom, L=Left, R=Right. Front Cover: Getty Images:
DEA Picture Library l; Shutterstock: Asier Villafranca r, Fedor Selivanov background. Alamy:
Mary Evans Picture Library 21; Altes Museum, Berlin: 14; Birmingham History Center: 11;
Clara Grosch: 8; CNG: 18; Encyclopaedia Britannica: 32, 33; Getty Images: DEA Picture
Library 1, 4; Joseloff Gallery: 10; LACMA: 19; Louvre: 6; Museum fur Antike Schiffahrt, Mainz:
40; Museum of Fine Arts, Lyon: 22; Palazzo Madama, Rome: 24; Private Collection, New
York: 29; Pushkin Museum: 16; Rijksmuseum: 31; Robert Hunt Library: 7, 9, 12, 17, 20, 23, 25,
26, 28, 30, 36, 37, 38, 41; Shutterstock: 27, Kizel Cotiwan 35, Mountainpix 15; Thinkstock:
Georgios Art 13, Photodisc 39;

Brown Bear Books has made every attempt to contact the copyright holder. If anyone
has any information please contact licensing@brownbearbooks.co.uk

Manufactured in the United States of America

CPSIA compliance information: Batch #CW16GS. For further information contact
Gareth Stevens, New York, New York at 1-800-542-2595.

CONTENTS

AT ODDS

CLEOPATRA Vs. THE ROMAN EMPIRE

Cleopatra (69–30 B.C.E.) was one of the most famous women of the ancient world. She fought to prevent Egypt from being conquered by the Romans.

* Cleopatra was well educated. Her father, Ptolemy XII, decided she would succeed him as pharaoh of Egypt.

* Cleopatra ruled Egypt for 22 years.

* At the height of her power, she controlled the whole eastern Mediterranean.

* She was richer than anyone else in the region.

* She committed suicide when she realized Rome would conquer Egypt.

From modest beginnings in 753 B.C.E., Rome had grown massively by the time Cleopatra became Egypt's ruler in 51 B.C.E.. For the Romans, controlling Egypt and its wealth was vital to the expansion of their territory.

* Ancient Rome began as a small group of villages on the Tiber River in Italy. It rose to rule the whole Italian peninsula.

* By the first century B.C.E. Rome controlled territory in Spain, Greece, and Turkey.

* Rome relied on its armies for conquest. In 58 B.C.E. general Julius Caesar argued that gaining territory through war was Rome's duty.

* Egypt was the last rich independent country relatively close to Italy, so it became a target.

CONTEXT

Cleopatra was born into Egypt's ruling family in 69 B.C.E. In fact, her family was Greek. Their ancestors had invaded Egypt over 300 years earlier.

The Ptolemaic dynasty took its name from Ptolemy I Soter (c. 367–283 B.C.E.), from Macedonia in Greece. Ptolemy served as a general under the Macedonian ruler Alexander the Great, who conquered much of Europe, Africa, and Asia, including Egypt. When Alexander died unexpectedly in 323 B.C.E., at the age of just 33, Ptolemy was in charge of Egypt. He became the country's ruler. From around 305 B.C.E., he became known as pharaoh, or god-king, like the rulers of ancient Egypt.

Keeping It in the Family

To keep power within the family, Ptolemy I decreed that rulers could only marry their immediate family members. The arrangement lasted throughout the entire dynasty as rulers married their sisters or brothers. Brothers and sisters were often deadly rivals.

FOUNDER: Ptolemy I Soter became ruler of Egypt after the death of Alexander the Great.

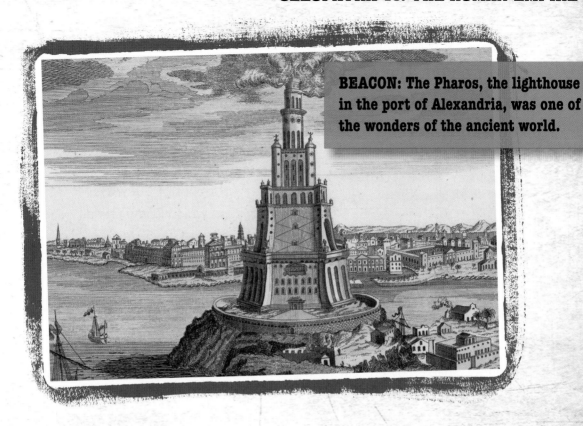

BEACON: The Pharos, the lighthouse in the port of Alexandria, was one of the wonders of the ancient world.

A Prosperous Empire

Under the early Ptolemaic pharaohs, Egypt grew into a powerful empire. It conquered neighboring Libya, Cyprus, and part of Syria. The port of Alexandria, on the Mediterranean coast, became the Ptolemaic capital. It was the most splendid and sophisticated city in Egypt, and had a famous library and university.

From Italy, the Romans watched the growing Egyptian empire with envy. By the first century B.C.E., the Roman Republic controlled all of Italy. Its territory

" A friend and ally of the Roman people "

Roman senate on Ptolemy XII, after he paid a huge bribe to Julius Caesar, 60 B.C.E.

> **"** In short, the city of Alexandria abounds with public and sacred buildings. **"**

The Greek writer Strabo in *Geography*, c. 23 c.e

stretched from Spain in the west to Turkey in the east. But Egypt and its island possession, Cyprus, had good supplies of the wheat on which Rome relied to feed its citizens. Rome was eager to add Egypt to its territory.

Ptolemy XII

In 80 b.c.e., Ptolemy XII (117–51 b.c.e.) became pharaoh in Egypt. His reign was marked by protests. Ptolemy looked to Rome for support. In 60 b.c.e. he bribed a Roman consul named Julius Caesar to have him named officially as a friend of Rome. Ptolemy's weakness

ROMAN: Julius Caesar rose through Roman politics to become consul, or chief magistrate.

FATHER: This wall carving shows Ptolemy XII. His reign was disastrous for Egypt.

became clear when Rome took Cyprus from Egypt in 60 B.C.E. Many Egyptian nobles turned against Ptolemy. In 58 B.C.E., he went into exile in Rome. While he was away, the nobles removed him from power and replaced him with his daughter, Cleopatra's sister, Berenice IV. Ptolemy returned from Rome three years later with thousands of Roman soldiers. He overthrew and executed Berenice IV. He reigned for four more years, but only because of the support of Rome.

Toward the end of his life, Ptolemy recognized that of all his children, Cleopatra would probably make the best ruler of Egypt. He groomed her to become pharaoh.

CLEOPATRA

Cleopatra (69–30 B.C.E.) was the most powerful woman of her time. She was the ruler of one of the ancient world's richest countries.

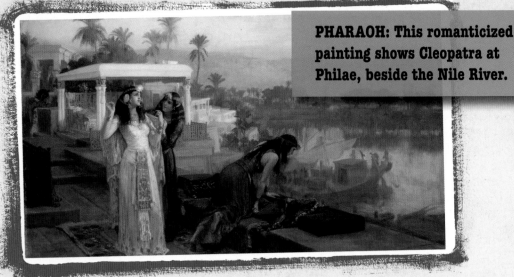

PHARAOH: This romanticized painting shows Cleopatra at Philae, beside the Nile River.

Cleopatra's full title was Cleopatra VII Philopator. Little is known about her early life. Even the name of her mother remains a mystery. It is clear, however, that Cleopatra was smart and well educated. In Ptolemaic Egypt, royal women were treated as equals to men and were allowed to inherit the throne.

Before Cleopatra, none of the Ptolemaic rulers learned to speak Egyptian. They spoke Greek, so they were not able to directly address their Egyptian subjects. However, Cleopatra did learn Egyptian and interacted with her subjects. She restored much of the territory and prestige Egypt had lost under her father, Ptolemy XII.

COIN: Cleopatra's portrait appeared on Egyptian money, which was widely used for trade.

A Skillful Politician

Cleopatra was quick to recognize potential enemies and allies. When Ptolemy XII died in 51 B.C.E., she became joint ruler with her younger brother, Ptolemy XIII, whom she also married. They soon fell out, however. Cleopatra wanted to rule alone, even though her sister, Arsinoe, sided with Ptolemy. Later, Cleopatra had close relationships with two Romans, Julius Caesar (c. 100–44 B.C.E.) and Mark Antony (83–30 B.C.E.). These alliances helped save Egypt from Roman rule.

> " Her beauty was not so striking that it stunned the onlooker, but she made an inescapable impression on people around her. "

The Greek historian Plutarch on Cleopatra, from *Parallel Lives, Life of Mark Antony*, c. 75 C.E.

ANCIENT ROME

The Romans had long envied the wealth of Egypt and were determined to add the Ptolemaic kingdom to their growing territory.

By 60 B.C.E., Rome controlled the Mediterranean Sea and much of the Middle East. In theory Rome was ruled by an elected Senate. In practice, power lay with the First Triumvirate. This was an alliance of the politicians and generals Gnaeus Pompeius Magnus, or Pompey (106–48 B.C.E.), Julius Caesar, and Marcus Licinius Crassus (115–53 B.C.E.). In 58 B.C.E., Caesar had himself named governor of Gaul, or France. He went on to expand Roman territory into Britain.

RIVER: Caesar crosses the Rubicon River in 49 B.C.E., on his way to topple Pompey from power.

RULER: When he became Rome's dictator in 48 B.C.E., Julius Caesar ruled as a virtual emperor.

Internal Fights

After Crassus died in battle in 53 B.C.E., Pompey seized sole power in Rome. In 49 B.C.E., Caesar led his army from Gaul across the Rubicon River into Italy. By law, Roman armies had to be disbanded inside Italy. Bringing his army into Italy was a clear sign that Caesar was determined to go to war with Pompey to gain power in Rome. When Pompey fled the city, Caesar set himself up as Rome's dictator.

In the summer of 48 B.C.E., Caesar finally crushed Pompey's forces in central Greece and seized control of ancient Rome.

> **"Today the enemy would have won, if they had a commander who was a winner. "**

Julius Caesar after his victory over Pompey, quoted by Plutarch, 65 C.E.

DEADLY FAMILY

Cleopatra knew better than to trust her brothers and sisters. In the Ptolemaic dynasty, siblings often fought over power.

As a member of the Ptolemaic dynasty, Cleopatra understood that her brothers and sisters would be prepared to kill her in order to protect their own power. Family tradition also meant that she would have to marry one of her brothers. Cleopatra first married Ptolemy XIII. After he drowned during the Battle of the Nile in 47 B.C.E., she married a younger brother, Ptolemy XIV. He died in 44 B.C.E. of poisoning, most likely arranged by Cleopatra herself.

Cleopatra's sisters also had violent deaths. Berenice seized the throne in her father's absence and was killed on his return in 55 B.C.E. Arsinoe later led an army against her sister, Cleopatra. Arsinoe was held captive by the Romans for five years before being executed at Cleopatra's request.

SISTER: After rebelling against her sister, Arsinoe was held at a temple in Greece until her death.

SON: This wall carving in Egypt shows Cleopatra (far left) with her son, Caesarion.

Loyal Allies

Cleopatra did have some loyal supporters, however. They included her two Roman suitors, Julius Caesar and Mark Antony. According to accounts, Cleopatra was also close to her favorite servant, Charmion. In contrast to her relationships with her own family, Cleopatra was also loyal to Caesarion, the son she had in 47 B.C.E. with Julius Caesar. She named the young boy as her co-ruler after the death of her second husband, Ptolemy XIV. She hoped that Caesar would also nominate Caesarion as his heir, but the Roman leader refused.

> " **The boy closely resembled Caesar in features as well as in gait.** "
>
> Roman historian Suetonius on Caesarion, C. 46 B.C.E.

ROME IN TURMOIL

» DIVIDED BY CIVIL WAR

Rome was governed by the Senate, a group of elected nobles. When Pompey and Julius Caesar clashed, leaders in the Senate took sides.

In about 50 B.C.E., Rome was split by a divisive civil war. On one side was Pompey, on the other was Julius Caesar. The two were former friends and colleagues in the First Triumvirate. They were also related. Pompey had married Caesar's daughter, Julia, who died in childbirth in 54 B.C.E. Pompey and Caesar had become sworn enemies in a struggle for ultimate power. Each had supporters among Rome's leading politicians and generals.

Powerful Supporters

The most important of Pompey's supporters was Marcus Junius Brutus (85–42 B.C.E.). He backed Pompey even though Pompey had killed Brutus' father. Pompey was also backed by the Optimates of the Senate. These were conservative senators who usually upheld the status quo. Their opponents, known as the Populares,

SUPPORTER: Although Brutus sided with Pompey in the war, he later became a favorite of Julius Caesar.

CLASH: Roman armies fight one another at Philippi in Greece in 42 B.C.E.

> **I assure you I had rather be the first man here than the second man in Rome.**
>
> **Julius Caesar, quoted by Plutarch**

wanted to challenge the Optimates. They backed Caesar. Caesar also had the support of Mark Antony, a general who would become Cleopatra's suitor after Caesar himself was assassinated in 44 B.C.E. Caesar's great-nephew Octavian (63 B.C.E.–14 C.E.) fought in Spain in 46 B.C.E. Nominated by Caesar as his successor, Octavian would later fight Mark Antony and Cleopatra and finally become the Emperor Augustus.

LINES ARE DRAWN

After their father died in 51 B.C.E., Cleopatra and her brother, Ptolemy XIII, became joint rulers of Egypt, but Ptolemy had other plans.

GOVERNOR: These coins from Syria show Aulus Gabinius, who sent his troops to Egypt.

After his exile in Rome, Cleopatra's father Ptolemy XII returned to Egypt in 55 B.C.E. with a Roman army of 2,000 infantry and 500 cavalry. The Roman soldiers had been sent to restore Ptolemy to his throne by the Roman ruler of Syria, Aulus Gabinius, for whom they were named the Gabinians.

The Gabinians remained in Egypt when Ptolemy died in 51 B.C.E. The throne passed to Cleopatra and her 10-year-old husband, Ptolemy XIII. As the king grew older, his advisors, led by the eunuch Pothinus,

TROOPS: The Gabinians sided with Ptolemy and Pothinus against Cleopatra.

worried that Cleopatra was trying to limit the king's power. Backed by the Gabinians, the advisors plotted to kill her.

Cleopatra Flees

When Cleopatra discovered the plot in spring 48 B.C.E., she fled to Syria, accompanied by her sister Arsinoe. By now, however, Julius Caesar had won the civil war and was in sole command of Rome. He was about to change Egyptian history.

> **The eunuch Pothinus was the most influential person at the court. Even openly Pothinus made himself intolerable.**

Plutarch on the power of the Egyptian eunuch in *Parallel Lives*, c. 75 C.E.

MEETING CAESAR

FLASH POINT » THE ROMAN TAKES SIDES

Ancient Rome and Cleopatra finally met head on in 48 B.C.E., when Julius Caesar arrived in Egypt in pursuit of his great rival, Pompey.

Pompey fled to Egypt after Caesar had defeated him in the Battle of Pharsalus in Greece in August 48 B.C.E. Pompey had formerly been a supporter of Ptolemy XII. Now he asked Ptolemy XIII for refuge, but his arrival put the young ruler in a difficult position. If he supported Pompey, Caesar might turn against Egypt. Before Pompey even landed in Egypt, Pothinus and Ptolemy's advisors had him stabbed to death. When Caesar arrived in Egypt a few days later, Ptolemy presented him with Pompey's head. Even though Pompey was his enemy, Caesar was enraged at the murder of a Roman senator.

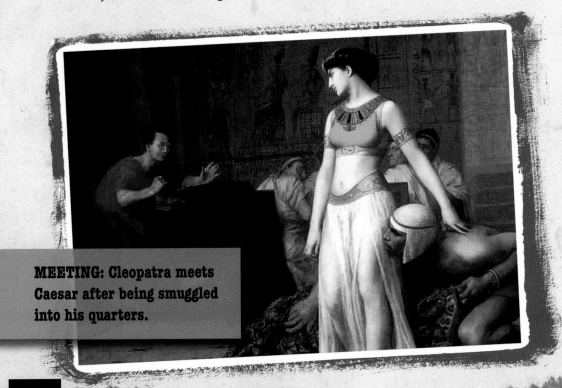

MEETING: Cleopatra meets Caesar after being smuggled into his quarters.

GRIEF: Caesar turns away from the sight of the head of his enemy, Pompey.

Private Encounter

Caesar decided to make a judgment about Ptolemy and Cleopatra's claims to power. He ordered them to a meeting. Cleopatra had returned to Alexandria from Syria. She wanted to see Caesar alone to discuss her survival. The night before the meeting, she had herself smuggled into Caesar's rooms, hidden inside a rolled-up carpet.

> **When Theodotus came to him with Pompey's head, Caesar refused to look at him, but he took Pompey's signet ring and shed tears as he did so.**

Plutarch, *Life of Caesar* in *Parallel Lives*, c. 75 C.E.

BATTLE OF THE NILE

After Cleopatra's secret meeting with Julius Caesar, she had the backing of the most powerful man in the ancient world.

Ptolemy XIII was furious. He and his sister, Arsinoe, raised an army and from August 48 to January 47 B.C.E., Ptolemy besieged Caesar, Cleopatra, and 4,000 Roman soldiers in Alexandria. Caesar sent for reinforcements from his ally Mithridates of Pergamon in what is now Turkey. Mithridates' army marched to join Caesar, giving him some 22,000 men. In February 47 B.C.E. the two sides clashed in the Battle of the Nile. The Romans won easily, thanks to their superior weapons and tactics. As Ptolemy fled, he drowned in the Nile River.

QUEEN: Caesar gives Cleopatra the throne of Egypt after his victory.

ARMY: Models of Ptolemy's Egyptian warriors. They were easily defeated by the well-armed Romans.

Fateful Clash

With Ptolemy dead and Arsinoe a prisoner, Caesar made Cleopatra queen of Egypt. By now, Cleopatra was expecting Caesar's child but in keeping with Ptolemaic tradition, she married her younger brother, who became Ptolemy XIV. Soon afterward, Caesar left Egypt for Syria. He left Roman soldiers to support Cleopatra and Ptolemy, whose Egyptian subjects did not trust their close ties to Rome. Cleopatra ruled Egypt—but she depended on Caesar's backing.

> **The eldest of Ptolemy's sons being dead, Caesar settled the kingdom upon the youngest, in conjunction with Cleopatra.**

Julius Caesar, *The Alexandrian Wars*, 47 B.C.E.

CLEOPATRA IN ROME

In 46 B.C.E., Caesar returned to Rome as a hero after establishing Roman influence in Egypt. However, he was soon reunited with Cleopatra.

SENATE: Caesar's power and popularity concerned many senators, who plotted against him.

Cleopatra visited Rome with her young husband and brother, Ptolemy XIV, and her new son, Caesarion. The official purpose of Cleopatra's visit was to make a peace treaty between Egypt and Rome. In reality, it was so she could continue her relationship with Caesar. Cleopatra lived in one of Caesar's villas and mixed with the leading figures of Roman society. Many people were shocked at Caesar's behavior. He caused more shock when he paraded Arsinoe, Cleopatra's sister, through the streets in chains. People saw this as a poor way to treat a princess. Some Romans were also concerned that Caesar might name Caesarion as his official heir.

MURDER: The plotters stab Julius Caesar to death on the Ides of March.

The End of Caesar

Meanwhile, the Senate rewarded Caesar for his defeats of Pompey and Ptolemy by making him dictator for life. Some politicians feared that Caesar had become too powerful. They were led by Pompey's former ally, Brutus, and Brutus's brother-in-law, Gaius Cassius Longinus. On March 15, which the Romans called the Ides of March, 44 B.C.E., Brutus, Cassius, and some 60 conspirators stabbed Caesar to death at the Senate. With her patron and protector now dead, Cleopatra fled Rome to return to Egypt with her husband and son.

> " People of Rome, we are once again free! "
>
> Brutus is said to have shouted this after stabbing Julius Caesar, March 15, 44 B.C.E.

ROMAN CIVIL WAR

With Caesar dead, Rome was thrown into turmoil. Cleopatra again found herself involved in Rome's dangerous internal politics.

LEGIONS: The Roman armies were the best fighting forces in the ancient world.

Mark Antony and Octavian formed the Second Triumvirate with Marcus Aemilius Lepidus. Antony and Octavian wanted revenge on Caesar's murderers. Meanwhile, Cassius and Brutus had fled to Greece, where they plotted to invade Egypt. In 42 B.C.E., Antony and Octavian pursued them. They appealed to Cleopatra for support.

Protecting Egypt

Cassius realized that Cleopatra could send reinforcements to Antony and Octavian. He tried to block the route to Greece with some 60 armed ships. Cleopatra's fleet set sail from Alexandria anyway, but

SHIP: Cleopatra sent a fleet of Egyptian ships and soldiers from Alexandria to help Antony and Octavian.

was forced to turned back by rough seas. Despite this, Antony and Octavian defeated their enemies in the Battle of Philippi. Both Cassius and Brutus committed suicide.

Mark Antony and Octavian were now the joint rulers of the Roman Empire. They agreed that Octavian would rule the western empire and Mark Antony the eastern empire. Back in Egypt, Ptolemy XIV had died. He was probably poisoned on the orders of Cleopatra. Cleopatra was now co-ruling Egypt with her son, Caesarion.

> " The Roman people felt at once a yearning for Caesar, and in consequence became harsh and implacable toward his murders. "

Plutarch on the reaction to Caesar's death,
Parallel Lives, Dion and Brutus, 75 C.E.

MARK ANTONY

Mark Antony, now the ruler of the Eastern Roman Empire, demanded that Cleopatra travel to Tarsus in Turkey to meet him in 41 B.C.E.

Antony wanted to test Cleopatra's loyalty to the new rulers of Rome. Cleopatra knew that her position as pharaoh was under threat, as she depended on Roman support. She planned her next move carefully.

MEETING: Mark Antony helps Cleopatra ashore from her barge.

Cleopatra arrived in Tarsus in a beautiful barge decorated with the finest silks and gold. Antony invited Cleopatra to eat with him, but she insisted he dine with her aboard the royal barge. She greeted Antony dressed as Aphrodite, the Greek goddess of beauty.

A Striking Impression

According to Roman accounts, Cleopatra dazzled Antony in the same way as she had dazzled Caesar before. Soon, Cleopatra and Antony were romantically involved. Antony was

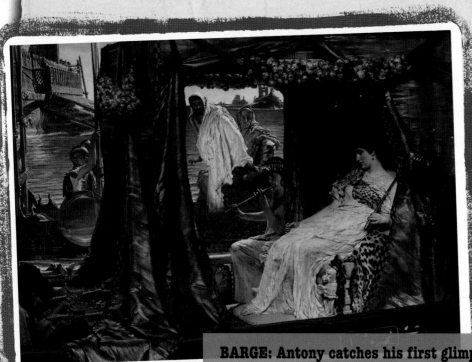

BARGE: Antony catches his first glimpse of Cleopatra in this romantic re-creation of their meeting.

already married to a woman named Fulvia, who remained in Rome. Despite this, Antony's infatuation with Cleopatra was so strong he decided to spend the winter with her in Alexandria.

Back to Rome

In spring, Antony returned to Rome. News had reached him that Octavian was trying to take sole control of the empire. Antony did not return to Egypt for almost four years. Cleopatra was now expecting a child and she wanted to continue her relationship with Antony. But she was also worried about keeping Egypt independent from Rome.

> " Plato admits four sorts of flattery, but she had a thousand. "
>
> Plutarch on Cleopatra, *Parallel Lives, Life of Mark Antony*, c. 75 C.E.

LIVING GODS

Cleopatra continued to rule Egypt during Antony's four-year absence. When he sailed back in 36 B.C.E. she welcomed him with open arms.

Octavian and Antony had avoided a civil war in Rome. In 40 B.C.E. Antony had married Octavia, Octavian's sister, in order to reconfirm his alliance with Octavian. Despite this, Antony returned briefly to Egypt in 37 B.C.E. and married Cleopatra. When he returned to Egypt the following year, Antony and Cleopatra lived with their children as a family. Octavian was not impressed. For Cleopatra, however, it was vital to keep Antony in Egypt to support her goal of keeping Egypt independent.

TWINS: This carving shows Antony and Cleopatra's twins, Alexander Helios (left) and Cleopatra Selene.

The "Donations of Alexandria"

Antony and Cleopatra had ambitious plans to expand their empire into North Africa and the Middle East. Funded by Cleopatra, Antony waged a successful campaign in Armenia in 35 B.C.E.. When he returned to Egypt in early 34 B.C.E., he and Cleopatra celebrated their victory with a ceremony known as the "Donations of Alexandria."

LAVISH: Cleopatra (on bed) and Antony (far left) enjoy a meal surrounded by advisors and servants.

Seated on golden thrones, the two rulers proclaimed themselves living gods. Cleopatra was Isis, the main Egyptian goddess and wife of Osiris, now identified with Antony. The couple's three children—the twins Alexander Helios and Cleopatra Selene and the infant Ptolemy Philadelphus—were made rulers of lands dominated by Rome. In addition, the rulers proclaimed Caesarion, Cleopatra's son with Julius Caesar, to be Caesar's official heir. That was a direct challenge to the position of Octavian, whom Caesar himself had nominated as his heir. Antony sent news of the ceremony to Rome. He hoped the Senate would approve of his actions but the Senate did not. Now Octavian was free to react.

> " To Cleopatra, Queen of Kings and her sons who are Kings "

Latin inscription from official coins made on Antony's orders, 34 B.C.E.

31

BATTLE OF ACTIUM

The fragile peace between Octavian and Antony soon collapsed. Antony divorced Octavia and planned to expand Cleopatra's empire.

Octavian was furious for many reasons. He believed Antony had insulted his sister, Octavia. He was also concerned that Caesarion might challenge his own position as Caesar's rightful heir. The fact that Caesar had appointed Octavian was a powerful means for gaining support from the Senators in Rome and from the Roman armies. Octavian also feared Egyptian claims on Roman territory—and the Senate agreed. When Antony gave Armenia and Parthia to his son, Alexander Helios, the Senate refused to agree to the gift.

BATTLE: At Actium, the power of the Roman galleys defeated the Egyptian ships.

LEADER: This statue shows Mark Antony. He was the real target of Octavian's war with Cleopatra.

Instead of starting another civil war by going to war with Antony, Octavian declared war on Egypt and its ruler, Cleopatra. His real target, however, was his former Roman ally, Antony.

Toward Battle

Both sides knew that whoever won the war would control Rome and all its territories. Expecting a Roman attack, Antony and Cleopatra

> " I made these wars for Egypt, and the Queen, Whose heart I thought I had, for she had mine. "

Words spoken by Antony, from William Shakespeare's *Antony and Cleopatra*, 1607

sailed to Greece, which Antony then controlled. They took a huge fleet of 300 Roman and 200 Egyptian warships.

In the spring of 31 B.C.E., Octavian arrived off Greece with a fleet of around 400 ships. For a few months, Octavian's fleet patrolled the Greek coast. They attacked Antony's ships, capturing his forts and killing his soldiers.

BATTLE: This painting shows Antony and Cleopatra being rowed out to their fleet.

Trapped in the Ionian Sea

Octavian gradually succeeded in driving Antony and Cleopatra's ships into the Gulf of Ambracia, or Actium, in northwestern Greece. He set up a naval blockade to keep them trapped. The land around the gulf was marshy and full of deadly mosquitoes. With no means of escape, Antony and Cleopatra's soldiers and sailors fell sick with malaria as the summer passed. Food and water ran out and many men deserted. By September, it was clear that the Egyptian queen and her husband had no choice but to smash through Octavian's blockade.

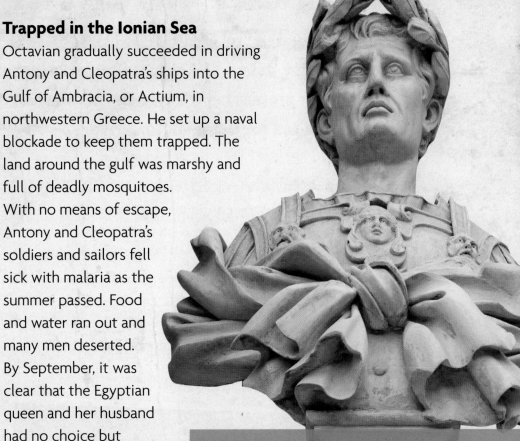

VICTORY: This bust shows Octavian, whose victory at Actium left him as sole ruler of the Roman world.

The Battle of Actium

The decisive battle was fought on September 2, 31 B.C.E. Antony led 230 ships into the open sea, where they met Octavian's fleet. The ships clashed throughout the afternoon, but Octavian's forces were soon in control. Cleopatra and Antony, who were on the same ship, managed to escape. Cleopatra ordered her ships to sail for Egypt. Antony ordered his fleet to follow, but their way was blocked by Octavian's ships and he simply abandoned them. The battle was lost.

TRAGEDY IN EGYPT

» THE DEATHS OF ANTONY AND CLEOPATRA

Following the defeat at Actium, Cleopatra looked for ways to protect herself and Egypt. She and Antony waited for Octavian to arrive.

Cleopatra knew that Octavian eventually would attack Egypt, but for almost a year she and Antony continued with their lavish lifestyle in Alexandria. Then news came that Octavian and his troops were on their way. Cleopatra offered to give up her throne if Octavian would let her children rule Egypt. He ignored her offer. Antony rode out of Alexandria to meet Octavian in battle, but he was forced to flee when his soldiers refused to fight. Angry and ashamed, Antony stabbed himself. Badly wounded, he was taken to Cleopatra and died in her arms.

SUICIDE: Mark Antony fatally wounds himself after his army deserted him outside Alexandria.

DEATH: Some experts think Cleopatra died from the poisonous bite of an asp.

Cleopatra's Suicide

After Antony's death, Roman troops surrounded the mausoleum in which Cleopatra had taken shelter. They held her prisoner there. Octavian treated her well, and allowed her to arrange Antony's funeral. He wanted to make sure she remained alive so that he could display her in his triumph, or victory parade. But Octavian refused to let Cleopatra's children rule Egypt on Rome's behalf.

Cleopatra knew she had lost her throne. She killed herself on August 12, 30 B.C.E., at just 39 years old. Many historians think she died from the deadly venom of a small poisonous snake called an asp, but no one really knows exactly how she died. With her death, Egypt became part of the Roman Empire.

> " I will not be exhibited in his triumph. "

Cleopatra on Octavian's victory parade, 30 B.C.E.

ROMAN EGYPT

With Cleopatra's death, over 3,000 years of Egyptian civilization had come to an end. Rome had gained the prize it had wanted for so long.

DEAD: Caesarion was executed on the orders of Octavian, who feared he might challenge his power.

With Cleopatra dead, the Egyptians offered no resistance to the invading Roman forces. In 30 B.C.E., Octavian declared himself to be the new pharaoh of Egypt. He ordered the execution of the followers of Antony to make sure there could be no challenge to his rule. Egypt became Octavian's personal possession. As a clear sign that Egypt was now under Roman control, Roman soldiers defaced monuments and destroyed official Egyptian documents.

Triumphant Procession

A year after Cleopatra's death, Octavian held his victory parade, or triumph, in Alexandria to celebrate his defeat of Antony and Cleopatra and his capture of Egypt. As well as displaying treasures he had seized from Egypt, historians think Octavian also forced the children of Antony and Cleopatra to march in the procession.

FORUM: Under Octavian, the city of Rome entered a period of construction of public buildings, such as those in the Forum.

Octavian realized that Antony and Cleopatra's children could represent a threat to his position. They could form a focus to attract Romans and Egyptians who opposed his rule. Historians think that the younger children were sent to Rome to live with Antony's wife, Octavia. After that, nothing is known of what happened to the boys, Alexander Helios and Ptolemy Philadelphus. Their sister, Cleopatra Selene, married King Jube of Mauretania in North Africa. The most serious potential threat to Octavian came from Caesarion, as Caesar's own son. Octavian ordered him to be executed in August 30 B.C.E.

> **I restored liberty to the republic.**
>
> **Octavian on his victory over Mark Antony, 14 c.e.**

AFTERMATH

With Mark Antony dead and Egypt under Roman control, Octavian set about turning the Roman Republic into the Roman Empire.

For 500 years after Cleopatra's death, Egypt was part of the Roman Empire. The valuable province was ruled by Roman governors and became known as the "granary of the Roman Empire." It produced huge amounts of wheat, which the empire needed to feed its rapidly growing population and its legions of soldiers.

The First Emperor

By 27 B.C.E., Octavian had made himself Rome's first emperor. He took the title Augustus, which had religious associations, and Princeps, meaning "first citizen." Augustus claimed that he was merely "first

TRADE: This wall-carving shows the sort of ship that carried grain from Egypt to Rome.

CITY: Under Roman rule, Alexandria continued to be a thriving business center.

among equals" among Rome's Senators but in fact he ruled as an individual emperor. Rome was no longer controlled by the aristocrats of the Senate but by the imperial family of Augustus. Under Augustus, Rome and its empire enjoyed a period of peace. In order to ensure that Rome reflected its political status, Augustus embarked on an ambitious building program in the city. In Egypt, Alexandria continued to be a center of learning and trade, but under Augustus and his successors, Rome's position as the most powerful city of the ancient world was unchallenged.

> " I found Rome a city of bricks and left it a city of marble. "
>
> Augustus, quoted in Suetonius's *Life of Augustus*, 121 C.E.

JUDGMENT

CLEOPATRA Vs. THE ROMAN EMPIRE

Cleopatra's reputation began to suffer soon after her death. Roman writers concentrated on her romantic relationships rather than her rule as Egypt's pharaoh.

* Cleopatra restored Egypt's prestige and many of its territories after her father's disastrous reign.

* She ruled Egypt for 22 years, despite being a woman in a world dominated by men.

* Cleopatra was originally popular with her subjects. She was the first Ptolemaic ruler to learn Egyptian and to travel throughout the country.

* Cleopatra was later blamed by Egyptians as being the woman "who destroyed the Egyptian monarchy."

Ancient Rome underwent great changes during Cleopatra's reign. Controlling Egypt added to Rome's prestige. Octavian's defeat of Antony and Cleopatra marked the start of a golden age for Rome.

* Octavian knew that defeating Antony and Cleopatra in the Battle of Actium would give Rome direct control over Egypt's great wealth.

* As the Emperor Augustus, Octavian led a new expansion of Roman power.

* The Roman Empire reached its greatest extent in 117 C.E., about 150 years after the death of Cleopatra.

TIMELINE

Cleopatra ruled Egypt for 22 years. She spent much of her reign making sure she had the support of powerful figures in Rome. In particular, she made alliances with Julius Caesar and Mark Antony.

Inheriting the Throne
In 51 B.C.E., Ptolemy XII of Egypt dies; he leaves his throne to Cleopatra, who is then 18, and her brother, the 10-year-old Ptolemy.

First Meeting
Pompey flees to Egypt, where Ptolemy XIII has him killed. When Caesar arrives, Cleopatra smuggles herself into his quarters and they form an alliance.

Visit to Rome
Caesar makes a triumphant return to Rome; Cleopatra causes a scandal by visiting him there with her husband and Caesarion, her son by Caesar.

51 B.C.E.   **49 B.C.E.**   **48 B.C.E.**   **47 B.C.E.**   **45 B.C.E.**   **44 B.C.E.**

Into Exile
In Rome, Julius Caesar effectively declares war on his fellow ruler, Pompey. Facing a plot by Ptolemy and his advisors, Cleopatra flees to Syria for safety.

Battle of the Nile
After being besieged by Ptolemy XIII in Alexandria, Caesar defeats the Egyptian ruler, who drowns while escaping the battle. Cleopatra becomes queen, with her brother, Ptolemy XIV, as king.

Death of Caesar
On March 15, plotters led by Brutus and Cassius murder Caesar, whom they fear has too much power. As Rome descends into civil war, Cleopatra flees to Egypt.

Death of the Plotters

With Cleopatra's support, Mark Antony and Caesar's chosen heir, Octavian, defeat Cassius and Brutus in the Battle of Philippi. Antony and Octavian divide the empire between them.

Temporary Peace

Concerned that Octavian is seeking sole power over the empire, Antony makes a new arrangement with him, including marrying Octavian's sister, Octavia.

The Final Battle

The fleet of Octavian traps the fleet of Antony and Cleopatra in Greece. The two sides meet in the Battle of Actium on September 2. Antony and Cleopatra are defeated, but escape.

42 B.C.E.   **40 B.C.E.**   **34 B.C.E.**   **31 B.C.E.**   **30 B.C.E.**

Fateful Meeting

Now ruler of the Eastern Roman Empire, Antony summons Cleopatra to Tarsus, in Turkey. The pair are soon romantically involved.

A Step Too Far

In fall, Antony issues the Donations of Alexandria, making Caesarion Caesar's heir and handing Roman territory to Cleopatra's children; the Senate in Rome refuses to confirm the arrangement.

Death of Antony and Cleopatra

As Octavian approaches Alexandria, Antony stabs himself to death on August 1; Cleopatra commits suicide on August 12. Egypt becomes part of the Roman Empire.

GLOSSARY

allies Different people, groups, or nations who agree to work together to achieve a shared goal.

aristocrats The upper classes or noble elite of a society.

assassinated Killed for political reasons.

blockade The act of sealing off a place or area to prevent people or goods entering or leaving.

conservative Committed to traditional values and reluctant to adopt change.

consul One of two elected officials who jointly ruled the Roman Republic.

dictator In Rome, an official who was given complete control to govern on his own, usually in a time of emergency.

dynasty A series of rulers who all come from the same family.

empire A large area of territory ruled by one country.

eunuch An official employed to guard the women's areas in the court of a ruler in Asia.

exile The state of being banned from one's own country, usually as a punishment.

gait The way in which someone walks.

heir A person who is legally entitled to receive someone's property or title after that person dies.

infatuation An intense, usually short-lived, passion for someone or something.

inherit To receive property or a title on the death of its previous owner.

malaria A sometimes deadly fever transmitted by parasites spread by mosquitoes.

mausoleum An impressive building that contains a tomb or tombs.

nominated Proposed to receive a particular position or award.

patron A person who supports another in terms of advice or finance.

pharaoh A ruler in ancient Egypt.

prestige Widespread admiration based on past achievements or behavior.

refuge The state of being sheltered from danger or pursuit.

republic A form of government in which citizens select representatives to govern on their behalf.

revenge The act of harming someone in return for harm they have inflicted on others.

status quo The existing state of affairs.

tactics The organization of forces on the battlefield in order to achieve victory.

triumph A parade held to celebrate the achievements of a military commander.

Triumvirate A group of three men holding power.

FOR FURTHER INFORMATION

Books

Dubois, Muriel L. *Ancient Rome: A Mighty Empire* (Great Civilizations). Capstone Press, 2011.

Jeffrey, Gary, and Ross Watton. *Cleopatra: The Life of an Egyptian Queen* (Graphic Nonfiction). Rosen Publishing Group, 2005.

Nardo, Don. *Julius Caesar: Roman General and Statesman* (Signature Lives: Ancient World). Compass Point Books, 2008.

Norwich, Grace. *I Am Cleopatra* (I Am). Scholastic Paperbacks, 2014.

Rinaldo, Denise. *Julius Caesar: Dictator for Life* (Wicked History). Scholastic, 2009.

Schecter, Vicky Alvear. *Cleopatra Rules! The Amazing Life of the Original Teen Queen.* Boyds Mills Press, 2013.

Websites

http://www.biography.com/people/cleopatra-vii-9250984
Biography.com page about Cleopatra, with a video.

http://www.history.com/topics/ancient-history/cleopatra
A page about Cleopatra from History.com, with many links to articles about ancient Egypt.

http://www.bbc.co.uk/history/historic_figures/caesar_julius.shtml
A brief biography of Julius Caesar from the BBC.

http://www.pbs.org/empires/romans/
A site to accompany the PBS documentary *The Roman Empire* in the First Century.

http://www.history.com/topics/ancient-history/mark-antony
A History.com page about the life of Mark Antony.

http://www.123helpme.com/view.asp?id=22702
An account of the civil war between Julius Caesar and Pompey.

Publisher's note to educators and parents: Our editors have carefully reviewed these websites to ensure that they are suitable for students. Many websites change frequently, however, and we cannot guarantee that a site's future contents will continue to meet our high standards of quality and educational value. Be advised that students should be closely supervised whenever they access the Internet.

INDEX